imagination & consciousness

written by uday dandavate

imagination & consciousness

author:
uday dandavate

editor:
molly pearson

design & illustration:
jung heo, savannah quarum

the poems in this book were inspired
by the meditations during the
covid-19 pandemic

self published in the united states
by the author
self publishing platform: kindle
direct publishing

ISBN: 9798846714311

San Francisco, November 2022

Dedicated to

Prof. Vasant Bapat

whose poems have nurtured in me
the   courage to dream and
to seek everything that is
truthful, elegant
and serene.

contents

●

Introduction

While studying people, cultures, and social imageries from around the world, I developed a keen interest in the common traits that unite all humans. This interest has led me to recognize two human capacities — imagination and consciousness.

These two unique capacities help us cope with negativity, pain, and sorrow. They help us heal, restore our sanity, and keep our ability to maintain equilibrium intact.

I hope that you will find my poems useful in expanding your consciousness and imagination. My purpose in publishing these very personal musings is to help you cultivate more resilience and mindfulness.

Thank you,

Uday Dandavate

roots

i can fly without fear
because my roots
keep me grounded
and safe from doubt

●

I am curious, open minded, and adventurous while exploring the hidden treasures of life. Fear of failure does not stop me from seeking out unfamiliar experiences, because from my roots, my strength and security bloom. In Roots, I welcome you to explore my roots — my upbringing and my culture — and my musings on them.

The fairest thing in nature, a
flower, still has its roots in
earth and manure.

—D. H. Lawrence

preparing for the future

in the midst of
pain and suffering
death and devastation
i see a sign
in the sighting of wildlife
in our cities

it occurred to me
that fear of death
forced us to retreat
into our homes
and make space
for wildlife
to discover
new freedom

it occurred to me
that we needed this retreat
so we could reflect
on what we've gained
and what we've lost
and create a new purpose
and a new journey

we now have
time to discover
the difference between

friends and friendships
wealth and richness
information and wisdom
connections and relations
goals and purpose
career and journey
success and growth
cooperation and collaboration
knowing and learning

we can't be sure
what the future has
in store for us
but for sure
the future is open
for reimagination

the future will emerge
from a shared imagination
that will evolve
through a dialogue

we can help
moderate the dialogue
we can help
frame the dialogue
by understanding
the dreams and values
that survived and evolved
and the fallacies that failed

we can't predict the future
but we can be
prepared for it

●

imagination and consciousness

consciousness
is a state of awareness
where we see
without our eyes
where we know without thinking
spread our wings and reach out
in stillness

imagination
is a state of transcending reality
where we see without our eyes
feel without stimuli
and fly without wings

imagination and consciousness
bring us
freedom
from doubt
judgment
and logic

the bravehearts

the future
belongs to those
who dare to dream

they can jump off heights
without fear
or assurance of landing on their feet
because they know
without failure
winning means little

the change makers
are those who believe
in their dreams

they can leap
even in the dark
and leave doubts behind
with open eyes
and a sense of purpose
because
they know they can
illuminate the path
for others to follow

●

they are brave
and they are kind
their dreams are shaped
by their compassion
and a desire to
change the world
for better

boundaries

prison sentences
inspired great leaders
with path breaking ideas

confinement creates
appreciation for both
freedom and boundaries

in pursuit of freedom
in fulfilling our desires
we disregard boundaries

we forget that
freedom is to be shared
in seeking freedom
we must not encroach
freedom for one
must be constrained by
others' right to freedom

the path to happiness
is not a joy ride
the challenges
the hardships
the pain
the suffering
and the sacrifices
create kinship

within the boundaries of kinship
freedom becomes
purposeful and meaningful
the boundaries to happiness
makes happiness attainable
an unrestrained craving
creates insatiable appetite

designers must define
boundaries to desires
we must cultivate mindfulness
and design a space
for kinship and co-existence

●

roots : emptiness

emptiness

the day
i lost my mom
i felt a hole in my heart
that i did not want to heal

because with that feeling
dawned a realization
that i was indeed
a part of her
until i left behind
an empty space
in her womb

that feeling
of emptiness
helped me
cherish her presence
all of my adult life
just as she had cherished mine
in her womb

the hole in my heart
brings to me
a sense of gratitude

i deal with my grief
with gratitude
for the space
she once occupied

a ray of light to live for

from where you sit
the darkness feels overbearing
the sun has set
and the moon is out of sight

on the horizon you can see
gentle ripples
bringing to you
a splash of light

reminding you that
when you close your eyes
you embrace a mix
of memories and dreams

a time will come
when a ray of light
will touch your eyelids
and remind you
that there is
so much more to live for

paradox

i have felt
lost
in a crowd
lonely
in a group
low
up high

insecure
in power

and also
confident
supported
fearless
and relentless
when walking alone
with a purpose

●

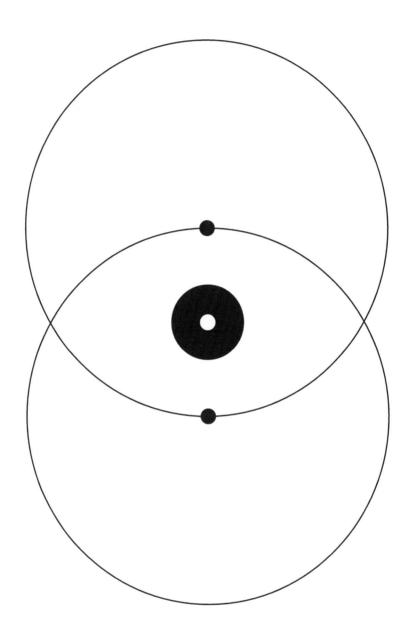

roots : NOW

NOW

if i try to
hold on to it
it slips away
and becomes
my memory

if i try to
prepare for it
it sneaks away
from under my feet

if i try to
live in it
it unhitches me
from my purpose

i wonder
if i can't
hold on to it
prepare for it
live in it
what purpose
does NOW have

i found the answer
in a state of stillness

●

when i am
free of intentions
and expectations
my senses
reach out
to the universe

when i am alone
in silence
i am sensing

in that state
i hear the footsteps
of our emerging future

i smell the aroma
of my memories
and i discover
the state of timelessness

in that moment
i feel present
and prepared
for the future

i am free
from anticipation

fear
doubt
and now
NOW stays with me

●

a prayer for democracy

every idea
has the opportunity
to play out

every voice
of dissent
has a place
of respect

winners
and losers
are just players

the spirit
of sportsmanship
prevails
over emotions

the passion
and fierceness
of debates
are limited
only by the boundaries
of civility

above all
the imagination
of everyday people
defines the contour
of the future
under construction
with the labor
of their representatives

i pray on this day
that in every heart
a thousand flowers may bloom
and the air be filled
with the scent of compassion

may our faith
in democracy
guide us
into eternity

●

autocrats

first they see
everything wrong
then they promise
to change our lives

once assuming power
they ask for more power
then they ask
for total power

once assuming power
they ask for more time
to correct the wrongs

then they ask for
even more time
until we stop questioning
the wrong

the best way for them
to remove the wrong
is to remove
the perception
and definition
of wrong

if we don't feel wrong
there is no wrong

●

they arrive
on our shoulders
they occupy
our hearts
they encroach
our minds

they plaster their name
on every building
every road
every song
and every story

until the only thing
they see and hear
is their name

if they had their way
they would write
their name
in every page
of every history book
and on every tombstone

when totalitarians
become blind
to the approaching cliff
the sycophants
fear to warn them
and recklessly
they speed up
to their fate

●

virtual doctor

i have a theory
no matter how much
you know about medicine

and about the human body
i know more
about me
than you do

i know
how i feel
how i live
what is possible for me
and what is not possible
i live with my body 24/7
you only have 15 minutes
to judge me

that's not enough time
to care for me
or to understand me
i am just a number to you

being healthy to me
means
not needing a doctor

●

if i could maintain
my health
and prevent
getting sick or injured
why would I need you?

i don't have the time
or the money
to be told what i already know

or what i know
that i should do

i know
my family history
i know what to expect at my age

if you don't care
for what i know
why should i trust
what you know?

you are predictable
you will prescribe medicines

or procedures
that i don't need

i know
that i don't know
what i don't know

●

i know
i could do better
by listening to those
who care

i would listen
if you cared
even if you are not there
in person

being there for me means
caring for me
having time for me
listening to me
not judging me
and helping me
to care for myself

and you can be there
just in case
i need you
in case of emergency

can i trust you
to be that person?

●

juggling

i was told
that a bird in hand
is worth
two in the bush

that might be true
but what i see is
life is more like
juggling balls

two in the air
and one in hand

you've got to
learn it
enjoy it
and never
drop the ball

●

beebo

i live where
nobody can reach
but you

i live
in your imagination
i am the child
inside you

when it's quiet
and you can
only hear your breath
and heartbeat
i listen
to your thoughts
and i feel
what you are feeling

i am here
to help you be your best
and to be yourself

i live in your imagination
where you can be free

with me
you can feel free
to be curious

to express how you feel
and to do
what feels right

as you add years
to your life
i will help you live
without the fear
of growing old

as long as
you keep me
in your thoughts
i will help you
open your mind
and your eyes
so you can
learn how to live
and love
with confidence

●

starting with a question

what would words be
without a language

what would language be
without thoughts

what would thoughts be
without meanings

what would meaning be
without a purpose

learning to write
is about
learning to think
and to make meaning
with a purpose

no matter
which language
we write in
english, spanish
python or java

the qualities
of a good writer
are curiosity
compassion
and creativity

creative writing
starts with a question

why?

●

statesmanship

don't make promises

set goals
make plans to get there
put your head down
and deliver results

nobody needs to know
how hard you are working
what is more important to us
is to see the difference
feel the difference

governance is not marketing
governance is logistics
leadership is not about
scoring high in opinion polls

leadership is about
steering the ship
through thunderstorm
navigating the crew
to a land beyond the horizon

statesmanship is not
market driven
nor does it thrive on
parochial emotions
statesmanship is about
breaking barriers
expanding horizons
and leading the followers
to embrace
a higher purpose

tone of voice

i am smarter than you
i have a solution
to your problems
follow me

i have learned a few things
i'm willing to share

consider this
i have heard stories
that i'm willing to tell
you might learn something from them

you have stories
i'm curious to hear them
i might learn something from them

i have questions
that i'm willing to ask
if you join me in my search
for clarity

balance

just like a tree
grips the ground
with its roots
as it rises up
and spreads its arms
we must stay connected
to our roots
so we can grow
unhindered

just as the tree
has a curiosity for the sky
while being rooted to earth
growing up
is more than growing
in size

growing up means balancing
where we want to go
with where we came from
growing up means supporting
our dreams
with our memories

roots : balance

growth

is growth just a measure
of business expansion
or performance?

is measuring growth
just about how much
wealth we accumulate
the people we hire
or the profit we make?

what does personal growth
look like in relation
to the evolution
of the universe

when everything moves
at its own pace
in relation to each other
personal growth is only
a figment of imagination

the truth is
we are all fragments
of the universe
each with our own
power of attraction
which keeps us in orbit
in relation to each other

●

harnessing emotions

emotions are
like a flowing river
when expressed
they stay pure

unexpressed
they are like
stagnant water
a home to
bacteria and disease
and turn our minds
putrid

just as a flowing river
contains potential
for energy
flowing emotions
contain potential
for creativity

suppressed emotions
are like a dam
about to burst
they have the potential
to harm and drown

in its purest form
a river is a nurturer of life
it can flow through
rocks
cracks
and boulders
fall from heights
and rise again
showering its surroundings
with a sprinkling of delight

once polluted
the only way to purify emotions
is to transform them
with a creative interpretation
let them rise up
like steam
and come back
to their purest form
like rain

just as dark clouds
bring us fresh water
we must learn
to transform dark emotions
into droplets of
curiosity and
compassion
and regenerate

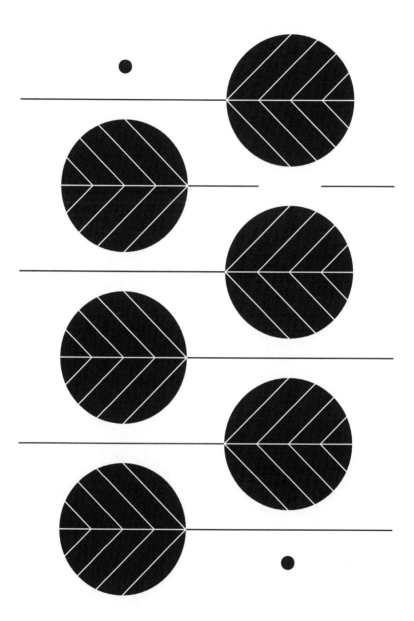

roots : cycles

cycles

life is not just
the time spent
between
birth and death

end of life is not
like a leaf
clinging to a branch
until it's time
to

f
a
l
l

there is more to life
than the life of a leaf

life is like a tree
a community of
organisms
that cycle through
life and death
to keep a forest standing

life on earth
relies on
the regenerative power
of the forests

sustainable design
is an ecosystem
of organisms working together

in a cycle of renewal
restoration
and growth

a leaf has a purpose
larger than its life
on the branch

inner thunder

when i'm engulfed
by a storm of emotions
i empty my mind
and turn my attention
to my breath

as i listen to the air
gushing through
my windpipe
i inhale with a force
stronger than the turbulence
then i exhale

i keep going
until i stabilize
my breath

in that moment
i hear the sound
of the ocean
on a dark night
i feel anchored
to the depth
of my consciousness

i sense the stillness
of the night
the glitter in the sky
and the smell of the ocean

i keep swaying
on the gentle waves
as the thunder passes me

●

return to the womb

when you feel
like you have hit a wall

when you feel
the path of righteousness
has brought you pain and suffering

when your decision
to follow the curiosity
and your instinct
to heal the planet
and restore people
to their purest state
failed to earn you a living
in a society addicted
to machines and medicines

when curiosity
set your imagination free
but you found
your wings clipped
by narrow minded toads

when your spirit was crushed
and your creativity stifled

when the only thing
that you desired
was to create
for your child
a healthier planet

do not feel defeated
my friend
the world my not be ready
for a healthier future
and an abundance
of inspiration
to live in harmony
with nature

your child still deserves
the cause you champion

maybe it's time
to go back to the basics
head home
where you feel
you belong

roots

unwind your mind
nurture your soul
give your body
some time to rest
so that you may feel
refreshed and prepared
like you are in the womb
once more

the future is
yours to make

●

my hearth

i was on the run
i was chasing a mirage

it took a pandemic
to realize
that it is my life after all
that i had to reclaim

i need to make space
where i can
just be

i wish
i could pause the clock
and take
a deep breath

in stillness
i can expand
my consciousness
and nurture
my imagination

i want to light a fire
and chill under the stars

i want to reconnect

with my soul
and my family
i need time and space
to rest
to heal
to regenerate
to reinvigorate
i need a hearth to sit by
so that i may reach out
to abundant
possibilities
of life

as i sit by my hearth
it connects me to my inner world
and to my friends and family

my hearth
is only one
amongst many
that are lit
in every home

together they create closeness
incubate love
inspire ideas
and set off a diffusion of
a shared culture

true awakening

in the pitch-dark
we can hear sounds

in silence
we can find meaning
more than
what words
can convey

when feet tremble
and lips quiver
the eyes convey more
than what we dare to say

the internet connects
but it takes a heart
to feel connected

video chat
enables conversations
but it takes the right question
to find the right answer

sages have
walked farther
and lived longer
in our imagination than
globetrotting executives have

with their glitzy presentations
and private jets

speed can get in the way
of a meaningful journey
a glaring spotlight can
blind us to the obvious

a persuasive pitch
can make us oblivious to facts

true awakening
can happen
when least expected

●

give it a shot

i have learned
to ask a question
even when
i may not like the answer
because an uncomfortable truth
can reframe my question

i express my beliefs
even to those who i know
are uncomfortable with them
because i know
that my belief
deserves consideration
in the spirit of accommodation

consideration of multiple beliefs
helps us understand
that there is more to know

than what we know
and there is another side
to what we see

i pay attention to feedback
loaded with emotion
even when it's hurtful
in feedback i see an opportunity
for improvement

in my ability
to listen
to observe
and
to distance myself
from my ego
i have learned
to slow down
and be quiet
so i can hear
my inner voice

i need it the most
when i turn a blind eye
to the consequences
of my thoughts

be curious
be open minded
be uninhibited
be fearless

to leave behind
lasting footprints
in the sands of time

●

grapefruit

when emotions
stack up

one
on
top
of
the
other

it's not the stack itself
but the thought
of removing a piece

one
at
a
time

that is overwhelming

if we treat life
like a basket of blueberries
with some sweet
and some sour
and start from the top
enjoy the good ones
then discard the rest

after all
what matters
is that one berry in your mouth
is sweeter than
all the rest in the basket

●

all you need

to be a lifelong learner
we don't need a teacher
we just need
lifelong curiosity
and an open mind

to nurture curiosity
and an open mind
we don't need schooling
we just need
to preserve our inner child

to preserve our inner child
we don't need
to act like a child
we just need
to follow our natural instincts

to follow our natural instincts
we just need
to follow our inner voice

the inner voice is the voice
if our conscience
is in harmony
with the universe

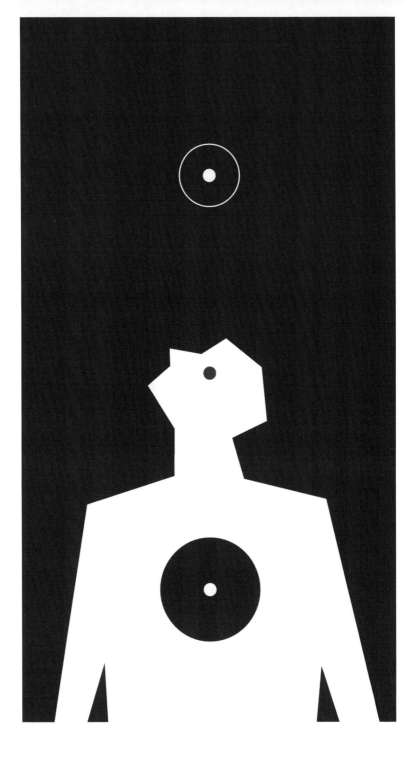

soul

my head
is filled with love
and my thoughts
are guided by
compassion

My soul is my purest instinct. It is home to my inner voice and my conscience. My soul resides in the deepest corners of my being, where preconceived biases and fear cannot contaminate my thoughts or impulse for action. Where my soul leads, I will follow, and when I do, I am able to fuel my imagination and creativity.

"Laughter is the language of the soul."

—Pablo Neruda

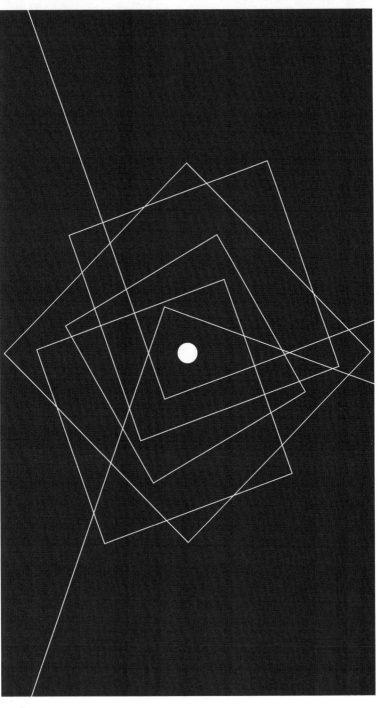

soul : my essence

my essence

my essence
is my freedom from fear
of the unknown

my curiosity
and my courage
whisk me into
the winds of change

my essence
is my imagination
and the power to listen
for the footsteps
of the future

i am not a dreamer
stuck in the inner eye
of my mind

i can see
and sense
inconvenient truths
and inevitable scenarios

my essence
is my resilience
i have worries
i have doubts

i know that pain and grief
are a passing phase
and i know
that eventually
i will recover
and regenerate

my essence
is my heart
full of love

i care and i share
because i believe
that a cookie shared
brings joy to two
instead of satisfying
the cravings of one

i have learned
that the most
authentic way
to build relationships
is from a place of love

●

soul

my essence is
an ever expanding
consciousness
flowing inwards
expanding outwards

i observe
without judgment
i rely on my intuition
my best thoughts
come to me
when i'm not thinking
but am just being
and allowing my subconscious
to connect the dots

my essence
is my persistence
on a journey of curiosity
in search of truth

i don't stop
at small wins or defeats
because the most fulfilling journey
is toward a future
that may never arrive
but is still worth pursuing
anyway

●

because it aligns me
with people that have
a higher purpose

i am just a proton
trying to build a nucleon
a minuscule particle
of the universe

●

soul

two worlds

while hiding in a bubble
i can't stop thinking of those
who live in a world
so different from mine

here we are
who have spent our lives
pursuing happiness
searching for meaning
sailing beyond horizons
reaching out to the sky
expanding networks
growing assets

i can't stop thinking of those
who have spent their lives
building our dreams
serving our whims
carrying our egos
feeding our greed
sharing our burdens
nursing our wounds

we lament when
we don't get more

they despair when
they don't get enough

we lose hope
when we fear
losing what we have

they have no hope
to get what they need
just to get by

we feel vulnerable
stranded in our homes
they feel vulnerable because
they can't get home

we wash our hands ten times
they are dripping with sweat

we observe social distance
they run our supply chains
they rush us in ambulances
they police our streets
they put out fires
they deliver food
they sit at cash registers
terrified and vulnerable

we are worried
how long it will last

●

soul

they are worried
how long they can last

i can't stop thinking
of those who live in a world
so different from mine

do we ever think
that to go upstairs
we push down
on the steps below

do we ever think
that to get ahead
we push back
on the ground below

without the steps
or the ground below
we could never
reach new heights
or walk very far

it's high time
we think of those
who we crush under us
and leave behind
because without them
we would not be
where we want to be

soul

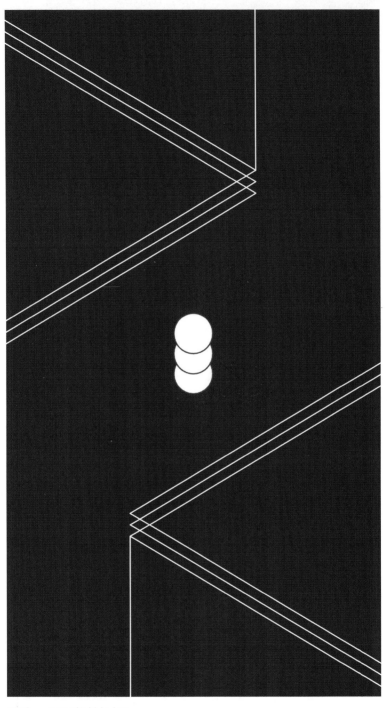

soul : possibilities

possibilities

i am curious about
the possibilities
that can emerge
from creating
a shared space
of imagination

in that space
we will create
comfort
trust
and a feeling
of safety

so we can
leave behind
our biases
shed our baggage
subdue our ego
lower our expectations
activate our senses
and breathe life
into the emptiness
together

i care because
i have been lucky
to receive
unconditional love
and encouragement

i care for those
who were not as lucky
i can sense
restlessness
anger
and pain
even when
it's not expressed

i seek
freedom
from doubt
and status quo

i believe
each of us has
a light inside
like fireflies
bright enough
to illuminate the sky
when we twinkle together
each of us
has a fragrance

together we can
fill the air
with inspiration
for caring
loving
and being creative

it's time
to heal together
to believe
in possibilities
emerging from
chance encounters
turning into
a shared space
for building a life
full of wonder

freedom from covid

he went in
to check his heart

all is well
said the doctor

not really
said he

for vikas' heart
full of curiosity
creativity
and love
was not good enough

a place
dedicated to
saving lives
failed him
with doctors and nurses
on guard

vikas'
indomitable will
to live life
full of passion
and compassion
could not keep
covid away

alas
the only way to live
is by socially distancing
even from those
who can save us

i would rather
distance myself now
mask myself now
so when it's time
for me to go
i can at least rest
in the lap
of my dear one

●

hope found

i offer you
a book of poems

share it
with someone
who is
hurting
and needs healing
heartbroken
and needs piecing together
lost
and needs direction
trapped
and needs release
unapproachable
and needs to open up

if they will open
only to a voice
from within
my hope is
that the poems
will speak to them

help them
slow down
hum
and tap their toes

my hope is
that these poems
will help them heal
have hope
and grow
from their core

●

magic smile

a smile is
nature's gift
to humanity

a smile has the
fragrance of a flower
sweetness of sugar
sound of the ocean
colors of a rainbow
and warmth of a hug

a smile feels like
a gentle peck
on the cheek
from a distance

a smile transforms
unfamiliar into familiar
skepticism into curiosity
a hesitation into a welcome

a smile has potential to
turn strangers into friends
put anger on pause
and stall aggression

a smile makes space
for a conversation
without words

a smile begins to
bridge distances
soften attitudes
and reveal
possibilities

even when
there is nobody to smile at
smiling at the mirror
warms the heart
and opens the mind

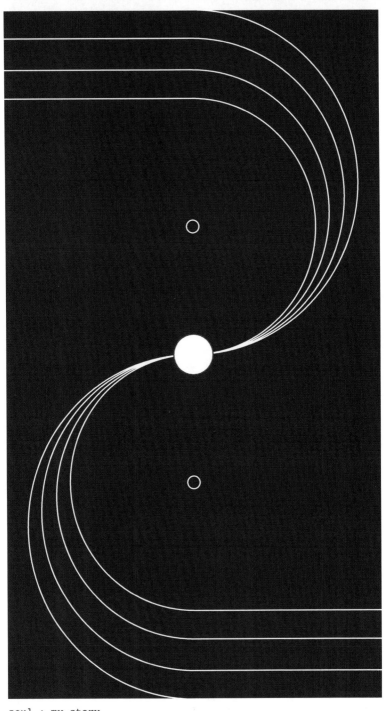

soul : my story

my story

last night
my friend said to me
now tell me your story
does it begin with the sky
or the universe
or your own soul

well it depends
on who is telling the story
and to what purpose

is my story
my pitch
a biography
an autobiography
a resume
or a part of
someone else's story

is my story
a dream
a discovery
a memory
or is it a
lingering sensation
for those
whose lives
i have touched

my story is
a story of
aspirations
adventures
struggles
wins and losses
and foolishness
we all experience

it is a story of
collective consciousness
a search for meaning
and an awakening

my story
is our story
of serendipitous encounters
and purposeful adventures
of the footprints
we leave behind
for others to
learn from

my story is
larger and longer
than the life
i will ever live
i am only a part of it
it's the story of eternity

it is a story of evolution
it began before me
and will continue to build
after i am gone

i will be in the story
as long as
during my life
i gain access to
the collective consciousness
and shared purpose
our purpose will live
beyond my lifetime

my story therefore
is the story of
purposeful, firm and fading
footprints
in the sand of time

it is the story of
my soul
seeking liberation
from the trappings of my ego
and from the barriers of fear
so it could become
a shiny particle in
the vastness of the universe
just like
the lasting illumination
of the fireflies
in the forest and
the stars in the sky

holding hands

when i stand there
staring at the sky
i feel i am conducting
a concert
and that
the changing colors
of the sky
are my orchestra

the exchange
of energy
between the sky
and me is
symbiotic

the interplay of
colors in the sky
and my emotions
has synchronicity

when i feel cozy
the sky feels like
a star studded blanket

when i feel philosophical
the sky feels like
a container
that envelops
my soul

when i feel sad
the sky feels like
a warm hug

when i feel inspired
the sky feels like
a palette of colors
that i can
dip my hands in
and splash all over
the canvas
of my imagination

when i am lovelorn
the sky whistles at me
whispers in my ears
and invites me to
just lay there
in its embrace
as its arms
wrap around me

the sky is
always there
for me
comforting me
inspiring me
cuddling me

we are in a
platonic relationship
the sky and i

in war and peace

the strength
of an army
is most evident
in the wars it has deterred

as much as
in the wars it has won

the strength
of the farmers
is evident
in the draughts
they have endured
as much as
in the food
they have produced

we must hold gratitude
in our hearts
for the sacrifices
of the soldiers
and the farmers

in war and peace
and in draught and rain
they remain on guard
so that we can let ours down

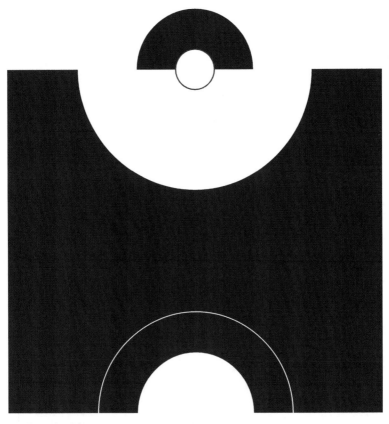

soul : duality

duality

the past year
has been good
and bad
and full of
paradoxes

i was liberated
from my ambitions
and yet
trapped in self pity and doubt

i felt isolated
from the real world
and yet
connected to my family

i met more people
on zoom and google hangouts
and yet felt exhausted
by digital fatigue

i found efficiencies
in virtual care
remote working
digital collaboration
and online shopping

and yet
felt frustrated
at being deprived of
handshakes
hugs
post-it notes
and white boards

i am grateful
for what
i have been able to do
with technology
and yet
i am convinced that
technology cannot
replace human interaction

during the past year
i paid my bills
by researching
human computer interactions
and paid my dues
to society
by writing poetry

in the company of family
i found comfort
and yet
in the confines of home
i experienced restlessness

i discovered
i can cover more ground
at a slower pace
be happier with less
and be a better person
without an agenda

in the past
i was driven to
help change the world
with disruptive innovation

in the future
i want to help heal the world
by encouraging
human capacity
for curiosity
compassion
and creativity

i miss the past
because i got used to it
and yet
i don't want the future
to be what the past used to be

i don't know
what my future will be

and yet
i know it will be
more humane
more mindful
more tranquil
more driven
by our humanity
than our technology

●

the queen's shadow

the queen
who lost her shadow
no matter how great
is the kingdom
she presided over

without her shadow
she will surely miss
being real
and human
under the glory
and sunshine
of her kingdom

when a shadows disappears
it's time to
rest and recover
so you can
rise to a new day again

life must go on
with or without
your shadow
with or without
the sunshine

when you wake up
you may see the sunshine
but not your shadow
you may feel
rain descending on you
but through your misty eyes
may you see
a rainbow
in the sky

precious moments

in the morning
i linger a few moments
in bed
close my eyes
and feel the universe
inside and around

when i take
the first step
out of bed
i pause for a moment
take a deep breath
then release

i reach inside
and pay attention
to my subconscious
in case it has
a memo for me

an epiphany
a memory
a lingering sensation
from the time
i went to sleep

i steal every moment i can
every time i feel rushed to
do the next thing

the pace i set
every morning
decides
what i notice
what i absorb
and how prepared i will be
to act with
with consciousness
and mindfulness

every moment
i find myself
lacking time
i take a pause
breathe in
breathe out
and then take
the next step

whenever
i am able to
let the phone ring
a few times
before i respond
i feel more in control
of my thoughts
and emotions

i have learned
that a pause
between thoughts
and actions
and slowing down
is the key to
moving with purpose
and acting with confidence

when i go back to bed
i try to spend some time
listening
to my breath
and my surroundings

as my breathing slows down
and the traffic noises calm
when i clearly sense
the silence
i am ready to let go
until i hear
the sounds of the
next morning

silos

trapped in our silos
we defend
our beliefs
and shun
fresh ideas

we live inside our heads
and bloated egos
shunning
the abundance
that life has to offer

we build walls around us
of identity and affiliation
shunning
the fresh air
that carries fragrance
from distant lands

we measure progress
by upward mobility
in the process
shunning the opportunity
to flow forward

expand
enrich
and eventually
dissolve
into the infinity of the universe
just like a river meets the ocean

from where we stand
the feel of the earth
to our feet
makes us egocentric
and blind to the fact

that even
the whole earth
is only a tiny spec
in the entire universe

that mother earth
stays in orbit
only because of
the gravitational force
created by
the planetary force
of attraction

to stay in our orbit
we must
care for each other

soul

flow forward like a river
expand our consciousness
enrich the shores we touch

only to dissolve
into
the infinite universe

●

soul

a life of wonder

imagine
an earthen pot
with a wide opening
and infinite capacity

it has a purpose:
to contain anything

that will fit its capacity
to accommodate

it lends its contents
a touch of fragrance
inherited
from mother earth

it has many functions
it will preserve its contents
and keep them
at a comfortable temperature
as long as it lives
you can cook in it
or even turn it into a filter

when you stir the pot
it produces blended outcomes
when you put it on fire
it leads to
magical transformations
of its hybrid contents

an earthen pot has
unique instincts
qualities
resilience

above all
when it has
served its purpose
it blends
into mother earth

an earthen pot
with a wide opening
and infinite capacity

is the life of
a curious
and open mind

●

kindergartner

those who know little
act like
they know a lot

when they know more
they act like
they know everything
and treat others like
they know nothing

they who know a lot
know that
they know
very little

and that they can learn
from anyone
who knows a little bit
about something

soul

the fountain of youth

more the years
i add to my life
more i feel curious
to start over

more the years
i add to my life
more i feel burdened
by the knowledge
i carry in my head
and at ease with the wisdom
that sharpens my instincts

today i wonder
why it should matter
how many years
i've added to my life

what matters more
is how much time
i have left
and how to
make most of it

as the years pass
my thoughts oscillate
between memories
and imagination

the pendulum
slows down
when doubt or despair
take over
it gains momentum
when curiosity and wonder
lift my soul
like a feather
floating in the air

on this birthday
i feel calm
the vastness
of the universe engulfs me
as i row a small boat
to the horizon

i hear the ocean
and feel the chill

the stars in the sky
keep me company
my purpose is
to expand my heart
and whistle gently
the song of love

attention is intention

i collect hidden gems
of meaningful moments
by paying attention
to serendipitous events
and counterintuitive ideas

i feel purposeful
when i envision a future
beyond my life

i feel accomplishment
when i set goals
impossible to attain in my lifetime
but still make progress
toward them

to move fast
i slow down
so i can get
my point across
i clear my mind
so i can rearrange my thoughts
and gain clarity

●

i pay attention
to the mundane
things of life
so i can notice
nuances that matter

i feel rewarded
when i let go of something
i want to hold onto

i diffuse my attention
so i can sense
more of what surrounds me

breakthrough ideas come to me
when i am not thinking
but instead am simply holding
the universe
in my consciousness
in a peaceful moment

auggie

you helped me
get in touch with
my purest instincts

you taught me
unconditional love

with you in my life
i became better at
observing
sensing
caring
and being present
in the moment

your eyes
are a window
to your soul
they make me
conscious
compassionate and
responsible

in your company
i learned that
the only thing that matters in life
is to be there
for the people we love

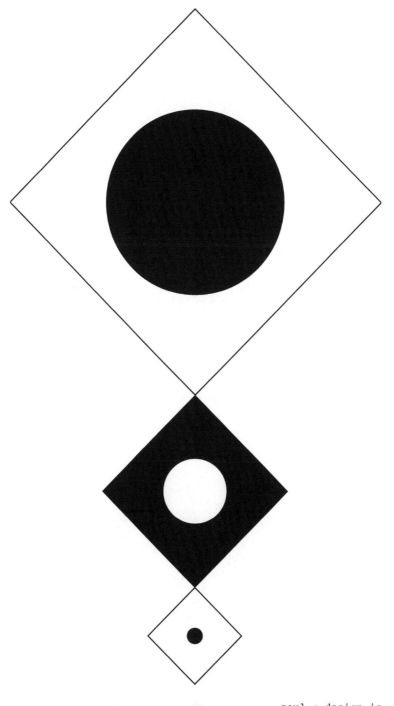

soul : design is

design is

design is an act
of imagining possibilities
used with
kindness
compassion and
curiosity

when we care for each other
build enduring relationships
and act with empathy
we bring imagination to
life with a purpose

good design
is an approach
to conserving
human energy
attention
time
and natural resources

an open mind is
a designer's workshop
where ambiguity
complexity
paradox
and problems
are comfort zones

●

conformity
self-consciousness
and fear of failure
do not hold
a designer back

good design needs
courage
collaboration
accommodation
and taming of the ego

the world we live in
is expensive
and the cultures we design for
are rich
life is complex
and changes too fast
to keep up with it

we must learn
to observe
to absorb
to adapt to change

the act of design
is an act of
co-imagining the future

ask as you design

ask yourself as you design

does your design
touch someone's heart
wipe a tear from an eye
put a smile on a face
alleviate pain
remove misunderstanding
help make a friend
dissolve anger
or enhance self esteem?

does your design
improve a lived moment?

does your design
serve a purpose?

can that purpose be
expressed in a poem?

idealists

i saw them
write their dreams

i was a part
of their dream

they lived
by their dreams

they shared
their dreams

they created in others
a space to
dream together

they held on to
their dreams

until it was time
to enter their dream

with a smile on their face

gathering

today
i tap into the memory
of the times we shared

i remember
the emotions we shared
exploring the unknown and
exclaiming "aha"s

and sometimes
when we hit a wall
we aimed high
and traveled far
to fuel our imagination
and to find a purpose

on this day
when i revel in those memories
and the imagination
that we created together
they bring me a smile

i want you to know that
i am grateful for
those shared moments
happy thanksgiving

thank you corona

it was fear of death
and not compassion
that led us to protect
the homeless

the pandemic was a lesson
it taught us
that left to suffer
and die on the streets
the breath of the breathless
and the stench of the dead
would carry the virus
to our air conditioned homes

our ivory towers
and metal fences
do not protect us
from breathing air
that we all share

●

during the pandemic
we hesitated to hug our own
and learned to care
for those who we considered
untouchable
only because we realized
that we are all connected
on this thanksgiving day

i thank nature
for breaking the news
that the only way to survive
is to care
for each other

●

complex problems

most problems
even seemingly simple
are complex
because

everything
is
connected
to
everything

and that makes every part
vulnerable to change

the root of a problem
often lies in the arrangement
of the parts

solving problems
involves rearranging parts
without disturbing the balance
of the whole

when the whole is dysfunctional
the solution calls for

patient
gentle and
empathic
improvement
of how the parts
work together
as a whole

disruptive innovation
is an adventure worth aspiring to
every once in a while

harmonious improvement
in the arrangement of parts
is how life's design works
all the time

extinction and regeneration
are part of life's design
and the real challenge for designers
is to differentiate between
extinction and planned obsolescence

the opportunity for designers
is to participate
in the evolution of
ideas
imagination and
life forms

with grace
elegance and
balance

who am i

the answer came to me
when thought outside the box
in which my ego
felt secure

when i looked at life
as a universe
of organisms
that work together
in a spiral of renewal

i saw myself
as a dot
meant to honor
the rules of growth
amongst
a community of dots
moving in a spiral

paul klee once said
a line is only
a dot taking a walk

with that framing
i am only
a dot on a walk
in a spiral of life

i am a part of a community
with the purpose
of spiraling regeneration

i have a family of dots
that stay with me
keep me from feeling tired
from giving up
or drifting from my path

in this journey
my ego is a burden
my curiosity gives me wings

compassion
a sense of empathy
for the other dots
in my universe

my emotions
both bright and dark
inspire my creativity
help me twinkle
and fill my path
with enough light
for other dots
to see the ground
upon which they step

the illumination
of our collective twinkle
has enough power
to create invitation
for others to join our spiral
of curiosity
of compassion
of creativity

a floating sensation

i'm feeling
a floating sensation
in the ocean
on a winter night
surrounded by silence

when my cravings
have no voice
there is no shore to swim to
or a horizon to dream beyond

the sound of the ocean
mingles with
the sound of my breath
creating a perfect symphony

i do not feel pressured
by my expectations
nor do I feel impatient

i am a reflection of the moon
in the ocean water
spreading a diffused and hallow
light to my surroundings

nobody cares
because nobody is there
to notice me

i still have a purpose
to be there
because I am meant to float
on the ocean water
swaying and smiling
as the night passes

i am floating
in the abundance of the ocean

my heart
filled with love

soul

a safe haven

when i hear words of
anger
hatred
bitterness
i move my attention
to my center

i insulate myself
i look for a quiet space

i pull down the blinds
so the scorching heat
of emotions
turn into a diffused light
bringing me
a soothing sensation

then i reach across
to the burning source of the flames
and look for a place
within the inflamed soul
that has not been burned
in the heat of the moment

we stay there together
wrapped in the comfort
of caring

while the flames
calm down
and fear recedes
the words of
anger
hatred
bitterness
have no home here anymore

in the scorching heat
of inflamed emotions
a caring silence
creates

a
safe
haven

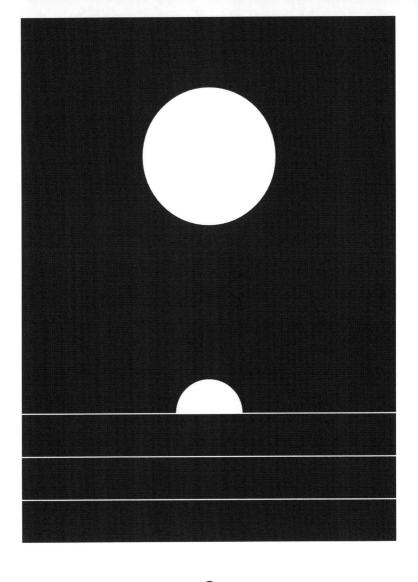

sky

the sky
invites me
to explore
infinite possibilities
and brings me
a feeling of
wonder
and abundance

The sky is my friend, philosopher, and guide. It inspires me to think big while teaching me humility. It invites me to reach for the stars while never forgetting the ground beneath my feet. The sky inspires my imagination and encourages me to never stop growing. No matter how far I reach, I can always touch the sky.

"Once you have tasted the taste of sky,
you will forever look up."

—*Leonardo da Vinci*

free

we were born to be free

to aim high
to aspire for a future
as far out
as our imagination can take us
to fly across lands
to follow our hearts

we must preserve
our freedom
and protect it from

masters
who bind us

education
that puts blinders on us

jobs
that dampen our soul

relationships
that trap us

knowledge
that kills our curiosity

beliefs
that blind us

traditions
that hold us back

emotions
that weigh us down

doubts
that slow us down

arrogance
that makes us reckless

pathways
that lack surprises

we are meant to be free

sky

hope

you will hear
your inner voice
when you pause
between the line

you will hear music
when you close
your eyes

you will see
a ray of light
when it feels like
you are lost
you will smell roses
and feel the tender touch
of a feather
when you set
your imagination free

your heart will sing
and your feet will dance
when you take a peek

through a window
for a home
without walls

sky : it takes very little

it takes very little

whatever little
i have had
was more than
what i have needed

in my firsat job
i made very little
and i did not know
how to spend it

my first home
away from home
was very little
and i did not have
much to fill it

i realize
that what i own
matters less
what is far
or transient
and hard to own
matters more

the skies
we can't touch

whatever little
i have had
was more than
what i have needed

in my firsat job
i made very little
and i did not know
how to spend it

my first home
away from home
was very little
and i did not have
much to fill it

i realize
that what i own
matters less
what is far
or transient
and hard to own
matters more

the skies
we can't touch

the rain water
that slips through our fingers
the winds
we can't hold on to
the rainbow
that is only an illusion
bring me more joy

what i need more is
that which
i can never
have enough

impractical ideas
unattainable ideals
unrealistic dreams

what i need more is
that which
i can not control

random thoughts
chance encounters i have
learned
to be the first one
to smile
at a stranger

it lightens the heart
creates curiosity
and sets the stage
for magic

attention

our experience is
shaped by our attention
from the abundance
of opportunities that surround us
we can only harvest
that that we pay attention to

obsession with being right

or successful
or with self gratification
makes us oblivious that the world
does not revolve around us

chance encounters
bring opportunities
if only if we pay attention

the world around
and the world inside
is more than the self
that we obsess about

the path to self actualization
does not pass through
self gratification

being curious
being alert
being attentive
cultivates awakening
and leads to readiness

for chance encounters
with opportunities
for growth

the pandemic was bliss
it brought us an opportunity
to pay attention
to passing opportunities

to harvest these
we must diffuse attention
from the self
and pay attention
to the world
outside and inside
only then
will the self
actualize

●

at the heart of design

at the heart of design
is caring
a designer who cares
brings
humanity
humility
humor
and harmony
to life

at the source of design
is imagination
everyone has it

imagination has
no limits
except
diffidence
fear
skepticism
and cynicism

imagination is
faster than wind
braver than the lionhearted
and unstoppable

imagination will
reveal possibilities

designing dreams

truth
is an illusion
a mirage

when i search
for truth
i find perspectives

i wandered
around the world
in search of truth

and discovered
that dreams
are real

more real
than the reality
that seems
so surreal
i searched
and searched
to understand
people's reality

●

and i found that
more than
reality
it is dreams
that matter

i found my purpose
in designing dreams
through poetry

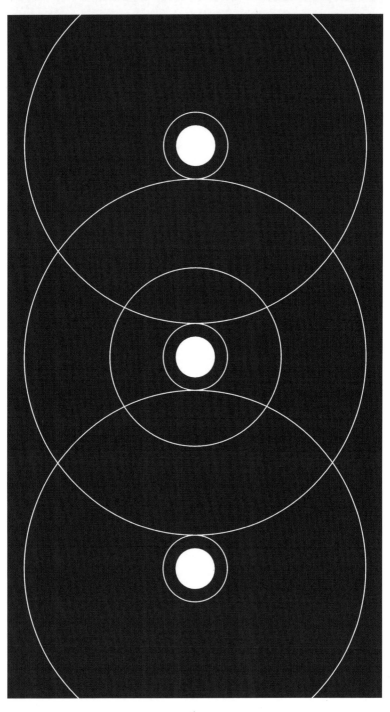

sky : glow worms

glow worms

the insects
that hold light in their belly
fill my heart with joy
like the stars in the sky
they ignite my imagination
fuel my curiosity
and fill the silence of the night
with festivity

glow worms cannot
fill a room with light
nor can they illuminate a path
the purpose of their light
is to create attraction

only the female belly shines bright
her brilliance attracts the male
she beams
they mate
and help their tribe survive

glow worms live
only a few weeks
but they have kept the forest
illuminated for centuries

they arrived on earth
before we did
and will last longer
than we shall

they hold light within
but have no power
we crave for power
but hold only ego
within in our belly

they live for the cause of eternity
we live for the moment

i have learned from glow worms
that a community of
illuminated souls
can fill the air with joy
no matter how small they are

or how short their life is
the cumulative effect
of enlightened beings
sparkles in the air
inspires imagination
and a life full of wonder

●

space

it's the essence
of emptiness
and content
of containers

it has a presence
that can be seen
only in relation
to its surroundings

space
separates
all things material
holds ideas together
inspires exploration
and contemplation
creates comfort
and accommodation
lives around us
and in us
lives in a vacuum
and in imagination
creates distance
nurtures understanding
and love

taking a leap
of imagination

to thrive amidst change
we must learn to
accommodate
adjust to
and act on
discomfort

and dare to imagine

numerous possibilities

harnessing discomfort
enhances creativity

●

harnessing discomfort

we feel comfortable
in the company
of those who
look like us
speak like us
and think like us

but comfort of familiar
can lead to
fear of unfamiliar

and make us feel
vulnerable
upset
and angry

change is inevitable

being prepared
for change
makes us
curious
flexible
resilient
and creative

being creative
means
being fearless
taking a leap
of imagination

to thrive amidst change
we must learn to
accommodate
adjust to
and act on
discomfort

and dare to imagine

numerous possibilities

harnessing discomfort
enhances creativity

●

winds

winds
are nature's gift
to life

winds
pollinate flowers
lift our spirits
and inspire our dreams

what use would
wings have
without winds

what would we do
with our dreams
without the wings
to take us
to our dreamland

winds
bring us change
winds
bring us turbulence
winds
bring us purpose
to be
wherever we can
and to become
whatever we can

just as
to live
we must not
hold our breath

to thrive
we must not
resist winds
of change

because
winds
are nature's gift
to life

●

petrichor

the smell
that accompanies
the first rain

evokes gratitude and hope
triggers primal instinct
elevates awareness and
expands our consciousness

petrichor
connects five senses
to the five elements

earth
water
fire
air
space

creating
a sense of unity
and bliss

purest instinct

no matter how much
you can learn
from the digital screen

to enjoy
the fragrance in the air
you've got to
go out there

let's make memories
while tasting flavors
sweet and salty
sour and bitter

do you know
a flavor called umami

let's go find out
just you and me

the only way
to understand
what pain
and love
and a hug
feels like

we've got to
step away
from devices
and experience
the real world

the characters
on the screen
have stories to tell
but they don't
transmit to us
the energy
and empathy
that real people do

you will never find
behind a digital screen
what you can
in the real world

love must be felt
by touching
awareness and expansion
of our consciousness
love happens in the moment

let's go find out
just you and me

i'm beebo
your inner child
your curiosity
your purest instinct

____

improve

is innovation
a craving of the ego
a benchmark of the creatives
or
an outcome of a mind obsessed
with disruptive change?

there is more to life
than an obsession
with innovation

not everyone can innovate
but everyone can improve

true joy of life
is in improvement

every single moment
we can improve

improvement is about
being mindful
responsible
and committed

to paying a little more attention
and putting in a little more effort
to make a difference

we can improve
how we breathe
how we think
how we imagine
how we respond
how we build relationships
how we make someone feel
and what we create

improvement
is attainable
and a sustainable goal
for living better

●

the messengers

it's in their nature
to flow
across
lands
cultures
and mountains

on the way
they create
energy

they inspire
curiosity
intrigue
creativity

they inject life
in every living species
they create hope
they bring
prosperity

it's in the nature
of wind
and rivers
to be open
and curious
and to flow
towards abundance

they carry
a profound message

that we are made
for a higher purpose
to nurture life

with

hope

energy

and flow

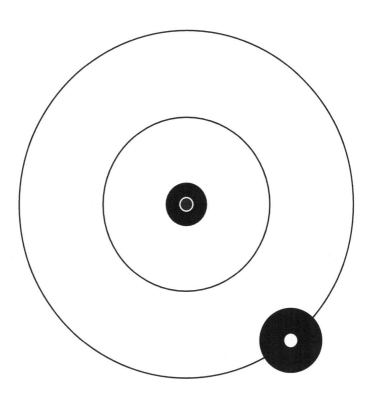

sky : what is dance

what is dance

an impulse
to express
a feeling of freedom
from the trappings of
conformity
from the inhibitions
of self consciousness

the sounds of drums
are an invitation
to push away
from the ground
float in the air
and feel weightlessness

the melody
is like a breeze
that twists and bends
the body
like the trees
swaying in the wind

the soul takes
a leap into the air
swirling around
like the leaves
flying all around
during fall

dancing dissolves
our sense of time
presence of ego
and expands
our consciousness
to the infinite universe

●

sky

the future starts now

now is the best time to live the future
we want to live

we spend all of our lives
trying to change the world
and then a time comes

when we realize
that it is more important
to reprioritize and live
the life we want to live

now is the best time
to live the future
we want to live

we spend all of our lives
trying to change the world
and then a time comes
when we realize
that it is more important
to reprioritize and live
the life we want to live
not in some imaginary future
but
right
Now

●

_____

you're invited

a glass half empty
is a metaphor for a life

yet to live
is an invitation
to fill it with
abundant possibilities
that make a flavorful mix

a glass half full
is a life already lived
the essence
of what i will become

i am a mixologist
mixing flavors of life
of life
to create

curiosity
delight
and openness

a glass half empty
allows for the aroma

●

to linger
and tingle
our palette

it allows the breath
to slow down
and the imagination
to rise

a glass half empty
is a space
for exploration
and creativity

dear ria

you arrived as the sunlight
was spreading its wings
and the birds were
taking their first flight
into the sky

you arrived when
healing and hope
were what the world
needed the most

you arrived when
the world was ready
for a change
as it never was before

your imagination will be propelled
by the winds from
india
switzerland
the us
and poland

you have inherited the beauty

and the composure
of the alps
and the magnanimity
of the himalayas

may your beebo guide you
on a journey of
curiosity
compassion
and creativity

may you always
stand for justice
and spread love

the future is
yours to make
dear ria

a design challenge

what does
a satisfied soul need?

how much more
comfort
how much more
happiness
how much more
self esteem

what do you provide
for someone
who does not
need more

what does
comfort mean
to someone
who has
embraced pain

what does living mean
to someone
who has accepted
the advent of death

what does hope mean
to someone
who never lost hope

●

what does the future mean
to someone
who lives in the moment

what does fear mean
to someone
who is fearless

what lives
in the imagination
of a satisfied soul

what resonates
with the curiosity
and values
of a satisfied soul

what do you design
for a satisfied soul

sky : audacity to dream

audacity to dream

we may be able to
silence a gun
with a more powerful gun

we may be able to
kill the enemy
with a bullet

but is it possible
to end enmity
with violence?

the land under my feet
right now
has a special place
in my heart

and my motherland
means everything to me

they both created a ground
for me to take flight
and dream

they both gave me the courage
and freedom
to take a leap
into the future

sky

as an immigrant
borders mean very little
to me

i pity those
who start wars
just to occupy lands
across borders

i pity those
who block borders
for those who want to build

a future of their dreams
on your land

i look at the sky

it has no borders
nor is the horizon
a dead end for my dreams

the sky and the horizon
are the starting points
of my imagination

i want to free up
my land
from the boundaries
of parochialism

i want to free the minds
of my people
to tap into abundant inspiration
for exploration of possibilities
across borders
and the horizon

we don't need guns
we need a brush
with which
to paint our dreams

we need
the audacity to dream
across borders

everyday

as a streak of light
says peekaboo
every morning
feels like an opportunity
for rebirth
to slide into a new future
from the womb of the past
that made me
who I am today

i wake up to the muzzled
sounds
and the smells
that invite me
to paint a new day
every day

i clean the lingering residue
of the past from my brush
as I put my feet to the
ground
unprepared
for a new day
every day

a warm smile
a good morning
and a cup of tea
are good enough
to embark on a new journey
every day

why wait for another new year
when every day is
another new day

●

show up speak up

in the vastness of the universe
opportunities are scattered
and life is too short
if we keep waiting for our dreams
to materialize

dreamers are those
who wait for opportunities
to knock on their door

imaginative are those
who bring dreams to life

dreams are important
they show us the impossible

imagination is important
it makes the impossible possible

to make the impossible possible
we need to show up
where our imagination leads us

●

we need to speak up
and invite participation
so we can unfold and unleash
the energy of our imagination
and gain momentum

the future
belongs to those
who show up
and
speak up

sky : adieu nightbirde

adieu nightbirde

you don't need
to brag about
your achievements
to be remembered

you don't need
to accumulate assets
for your loved ones
to cherish your memory

you don't need
to waste life
fighting battles
to feel victorious

life is short
live it
feel it
and become inspired
to write a song

you should not wait
until life
isn't hard anymore
before you decide
to be happy.
it's ok
says nightbirde

"When we stop fighting with ourselves, we aren't creating anymore conflict in our mind. Then our mind can for the first time relax and be still. Then for the first time our consciousness can become whole and unfragmented. Then total attention can be given to all of our thoughts and feelings. And then there will be found a gentleness and a goodness in us that can embrace all that has been given in the world. Then a deep love for everything will be the result of this deep attention. For this total attention, this soft and pure consciousness that we are, is nothing but Love itself."

—*Jiddu Krishnamurti*

"Imagination is more important than knowledge. For knowledge is limited to all we now know and understand, while imagination embraces the entire world, and all there ever will be to know and understand."

—*Albert Einstein*

UDAY DANDAVATE is a design activist, poet, and an ethnographer of social imagination. Uday has traveled extensively around the world, studying and connecting with all  kinds of people and cultures, and watching and participating as they change over time. In his professional capacity, as well as through blogging, teaching, speaking, and facilitating, Uday provokes fresh perspectives that help to humanize technologies and democratize design. During Covid-19 pandemic Uday published an evocative collection of poems, "a window for a home without walls," that help communicate values and sensitivities about life, imagination and design. in 2021 he published an illustrated book "Finding Your Beebo" to encourage a dialogue between parents and children about the importance of preserving our inner child.

Made in the USA
Coppell, TX
06 December 2022

88027127R00103